ABC of Golf

© 2021 by Alexander Jordan

All rights reserved. No part of this book may be reproduced or transmitted in any form or by any means, electronic, mechanical, photocopying, recording, or otherwise without prior written permission.

ISBN 9798593335425

This book belongs to _____.

A is for Albatross

Three under par. It's rarely seen!

B is for Ball

Yellow, blue, white, and green.

C is for Cart

The best way to get around.

D is for Divot

Make sure you pat it back down.

E is for Eagle

That's two under. I'd be proud.

F is for FORE!

Yell it out nice and loud!

G is for Grip

Get those hands in place.

H is for Hole-in-One

It's also called an ace.

I is for Iron

Usually numbered from 3 to 9.

J is for Jungle

Best to take a drop sometimes.

K is for Kitty Litter

The sand trap, bunker, or the beach.

L is for Lost

Sometimes hiding or out of reach.

M is for Mulligan

Just have another go.

N is for Nicklaus

Jack won 18 majors. Whoa!

O is for Outfit

Make sure you're dressed the part!

P is for Putting

Getting it right is an art.

Q is for Quiet

"Let me know if I am distracting you."

Let the player concentrate.

R is for Rake

Leave the bunker in a perfect state.

S is for Snowman

Scoring eight. That's not good.

T is for Tee

Some are plastic, some are wood.

U is for Umbrella

If it rains, put it up.

V is for Victory Lap

When the ball rolls around the cup.

W is for Water

I don't want to hear a splash!

X is for X-Out

You can save a bit of cash.

Y is for Yards

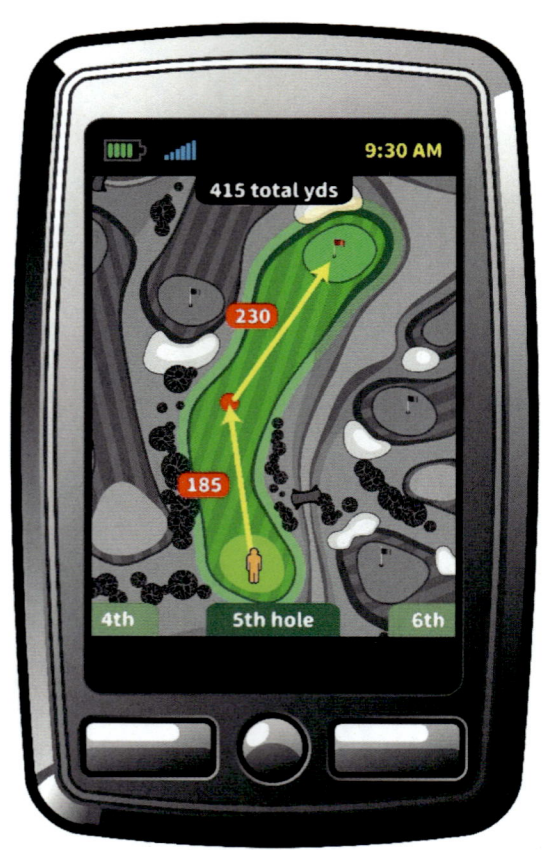

How far have we got?

Z is for Zinger

Now that's a healthy shot.

Made in the USA
Monee, IL
23 May 2021